Jhonny R. Ross

THE GOOD
EXECUTIVE ASSISTANT

PRACTICAL GUIDE

TO MASTERING KEY SKILLS

Dedicated to my mother and my father.

It is impossible to express in words how much they have meant to me. This dedication is only a modest attempt to convey the deep gratitude and love I feel for them. They have been not only my parents, but also my mentors, inspirers and the most extraordinary supporters I could have wished for in life.

From the very beginning, they have shaped my existence with core values such as love, kindness and determination. They instilled in me a sense of responsibility and respect for others, teaching me that success is the result of hard work and integrity.

They have supported me at every stage of my growth, encouraging me to pursue my dreams and overcome challenges with courage. They instilled in me confidence in my abilities and taught me to believe in myself.

Their words of wisdom, invaluable advice and constant presence in my adventures have made my journey of growth and personal fulfillment possible. They were my first teachers and guides.

This book, dedicated to them, is a small tribute to their extraordinary influence in my life. Every page, every word, every idea is influenced by their love and wisdom. It is a way to celebrate their legacy and share it with the world.

I hope this book can be a small demonstration of how much I appreciate all they have done for me.

Thank you, dear parents, for all that you are and all that you have done. My love and gratitude for you are eternal.

With infinite affection and gratitude.

Dear and motivated reader,

I welcome you to this exciting journey toward excellence as an executive assistant. If you have taken this book in your hands, it is clear that you have already taken an important step toward your goal of becoming an outstanding executive assistant. I want to begin this journey of ours by telling you that you have made the right choice because you will be surprised at how rewarding and fulfilling working as a successful executive assistant can be..

I want to share with you all that I have learned over the years in my role as secretary. I am convinced that an executive assistant is not just an assistant, but a real key figure in any work environment. Are you ready to start this journey with me? Great!

Working as a successful executive assistant is more than just a job; it is an opportunity to leave a positive imprint in any work environment. If you want to be a pillar, a beacon of efficiency and professionalism for your company or employer, you are in the right place. But know that your role is not limited to administrative tasks. You are the beating heart of the office, the person who keeps everything moving, the valuable resource that makes life easier for everyone else.

I have devoted years of my life to perfecting the art of the executive assistant. I have gone through ups and downs, faced challenges and celebrated successes. And now, I want to share everything I have learned with you. This is not just a book, but a practical guide that will take you step by step on your path to professional growth and success.

Over the course of the next few pages, you will discover not only the practical skills and abilities you need to excel as an executive assistant, but also the mindset and philosophy that will enable you to stand out. You will be surprised at how rewarding and fulfilling it can be to reach the top of your career in this role.

An executive assistant is not just an assistant. She is an advisor, a problem solver, a coordinator, a pillar of support for the entire team. You will be the person everyone turns to for crucial information, to get help when they are stuck, and to make sure everything runs smoothly. Your role is critically important, and I firmly believe that you can do it successfully.

So get ready to transform yourself into an amazing executive assistant!

We will explore together the skills, knowledge, and mindset needed to become the executive assistant everyone talks about with admiration. The path may be challenging, but it is also extremely rewarding. I hope you are excited and ready to begin this incredible journey together!

Buckle up and get ready to become the executive assistant everyone will talk about with admiration.

Awesome! Let's get started right now!

SUMMARY

Chapter 1: The Art of Communication
(page 12)

One of the most important skills for an executive assistant is the ability to communicate effectively. You will learn how to write flawless e-mails, handle phone calls professionally, and establish positive working relationships with colleagues and superiors.

Chapter 2: Organization and Time Management.
(page 32)

No other skill is more crucial to a successful executive assistant. I will teach you how to plan your day, manage deadlines, and keep your office running like a Swiss watch.

Chapter 3: Mastery in Technology
(page 39)

Today, technology is our best friend. You'll discover how to master the most useful applications and software to increase your productivity and simplify your office work.

Chapter 4: Problem Solving and Decision Making. (page 45)

Executive assistants are often involved in problem solving and decision making. I will give you the tools to approach difficult situations with confidence and determination.

Chapter 5: Managing Stress and Maintaining a Work-Life Balance (page 52)

The job of executive assistant can be very demanding, but maintaining a balance between work and personal life is essential. You will learn techniques for managing stress and enjoying your life outside the office.

Chapter 6: Professional Growth and Continuing Development. (page 60)

Your career as an executive assistant is a constantly evolving path. I will explain why constantly improving your skills will help you advance in your career.

Chapter 7: The Business Card
(page 64)

It is important to note that appearance should not be used to judge a person's worth, but it is undeniable that it is a crucial aspect for an executive assistant working in a company because it is his or her first calling card. The way you physically present yourself greatly affects others' perception of you and the company where you work.

Chapter 8: Love your job
(page 69)

We will explore why love of work is so vital for executive assistants and the impact it can have on their health and personal lives.

Chapter 9: Multitasking
(page 74)

The importance of multitasking for an executive assistant and some techniques for mastering this skill.

Chapter 10:The Art of Putting Frosting on.
(page 79)

The art of putting icing in your work: standing out with excellence through attention to detail and dedication to your work.

Chapter 11: Stories of Success
(page 86)

In this chapter, I will share true stories of executive assistants who have achieved success. They will be inspiring and demonstrate that you can achieve any goal you set for yourself.

At the end of each chapter, you will find practical tips and suggestions that you can put into action immediately to improve your skills. Remember that becoming an outstanding executive assistant requires commitment and constant improvement, but the results will be rewarding.

Chapter 1

The Art of Communication

Communication is, without a doubt, the keystone of our role as executive assistants. It is like the common thread that holds the fabric of the office with the company together. Imagine communication as a bridge between you and the world outside, between you and your colleagues, between you and your superiors. It is this connection that enables you to be not just a simple task performer, but a central figure in creating positive relationships, achieving effective results, and working in harmony with all the people you encounter in your job.

In this chapter, we will open the door to a world of knowledge and skills that will transform you into a true expert in communication. You will discover how effectively your ability to communicate can positively affect every aspect of your career.

Communication as the key to positive relationships

Imagine working in an environment where every message is clearly communicated, where there is mutual trust between you, your colleagues and your superiors. This environment fosters collaboration, creativity and productivity. Effective communication is the key to building positive relationships in the office. When you express yourself clearly and empathetically, you convey trust and open the door to mutual understanding.

For example, suppose you need to communicate an urgent deadline to a colleague. Effective communication involves not only informing your colleague of the deadline, but also sharing the resources and support needed to achieve that goal. This not only relieves your colleague's stress but also creates a solid foundation for positive future collaboration.

Communication needed to achieve effective results

Clear communication is the high road to effective results. Imagine you are responsible for managing a complex project. If you can effectively communicate goals, deadlines and expectations to your team members, they will be able to work more efficiently. In addition, continuous communication will enable you to monitor the status of the project, make changes if necessary, and ensure that everything is going according to plan.

Communication to work in harmony

In the corporate world, collaboration is fundamental. No one works in a silo, and communication is what enables you to coordinate with your colleagues and superiors. When everyone clearly understands tasks and expectations, teamwork becomes more effective. Communication is the lubricant that keeps the wheels of the organization moving without any friction.

For example, in a job environment, open and honest communication is essential to deal with any problems or misunderstandings in a constructive way. When people feel free to express their opinions and concerns, it is more likely that effective solutions can be found.

In this chapter, we will explore the fundamentals of effective communication, including verbal and written communication, managing emotions, and the skills needed to actively listen. You will learn how to apply these skills in your daily work to create a harmonious work environment, achieve positive results, and build strong relationships with your colleagues and superiors. Communication is your main tool, and with the right skills, you can use it to drive you to success as an outstanding executive assistant.

Perfect Written Communication

Written communication is central to success as an executive assistant. Your emails and written documents represent not only you, but also the company you work for. Here are some tips and examples to help you perfect this critical skill:

Flawless e-mails

Clear and informative subject line: Imagine you have to write an e-mail to your supervisor about an urgent project. A subject line like "Request for Approval of XYZ Project By 10/10" is much more effective than a vague one like "XYZ Project." The clear subject line immediately indicates the nature and urgency of the message.

Appropriate greeting: Always begin with a professional greeting, using the person's name if it is appropriate. For example, "Dear [Recipient's Name]" or "Hello [Recipient's Name]." Avoid overly informal greetings such as "Hello" unless you have a very close relationship with the recipient.

Professional tone: Maintain a professional and respectful tone throughout the message. Avoid sarcasm, informal language, or personal comments that are not closely related to the topic of the e-mail.

Clear and concise message: Clarity is essential. Explain the reason for the e-mail in a direct and concise manner. Use short paragraphs to break down concepts and make reading easier. For example, if you are writing a project status report, organize it into clear sections such as "Project Goals," "Milestones Completed," and "Next Steps."

Professional Signature: Conclude your e-mail with a professional signature that includes your name, your title, the company where you work, and your contact information. Here is an example:

Sincerely
[Your Name]
Executive Assistant
[Company Name]
Phone: [Your phone number]

Spelling and Grammar Review: Before sending your e-mail, proofread it carefully for spelling or grammatical errors. You may also use auto- correct tools, but do not rely on them completely.

Here is an example of a well-structured e-mail:

"Subject: Request for Approval of Project XYZ By 10/10

Hello [Recipient's Name],

I hope you are having a good day. I am writing to request your approval for the XYZ project. We have been working diligently to achieve all the planned milestones and are ready to proceed with the next phase.

In the attached document you will find a detailed overview of the current status of the project, along with the team's recommendations. Please take a moment to review it. If you have any questions or comments, I will be happy to address any concerns you may have.

I greatly appreciate your input and guidance in this project. Your feedback is extremely important to us, and your approval will allow us to move forward with confidence.

Sincerely.
[Your Name]
Executive Assistant
[Company Name]
Phone: [Your phone number]"

This example demonstrates how effective written communication can be clear, courteous, and informative. Keep practicing and practicing these principles to hone your skills in writing flawless e-mails.

Interpersonal Relations and Verbal Communication

Interpersonal relationships are a cornerstone for success in any role, but they are especially crucial for an executive assistant. Your skill at building and maintaining positive relationships with colleagues, superiors, and other key figures in the organization is one of your most valuable assets. In this section, we will explore how to cultivate and manage effective interpersonal relationships.

Creating positive working relationships

Imagine that you are surrounded by colleagues and superiors with whom you feel comfortable, with whom it is easy to collaborate and communicate. This is the result of positive working relationships that you have helped build.

Here are some strategies for how to do that:

- Show Respect: Treat others with respect and courtesy. Use kind words and avoid making dismissive or critical comments. Even in difficult situations, try to remain calm and composed. Respect is a keystone for building successful interpersonal relationships. As an executive assistant, your skill in treating others with respect is essential to creating a positive and constructive workplace.

- Be Kind: Make kindness your best weapon for working in harmony and peace of mind. In my 20-year career, I have received so many compliments because of my kindness. Kindness is a powerful resource for creating a harmonious and peaceful workplace. When challenges or tensions arise, resorting to kindness can be the key to successfully resolving them. Breathing deeply and mentally counting to three before responding in stressful situations can help you remain calm and respond with kindness instead of reacting impulsively. Kindness is a valued quality in any career, and can lead to receiving praise and respect from colleagues and superiors. When you ask for something, the use of words such as "please" and "please" shows respect and consideration toward others. This form of positive communication encourages positive responses and contributes to a healthy and productive workplace. In addition, kindness not only improves workplace relationships, but can also positively influence the corporate culture as a whole. When individuals behave kindly, they create a ripple effect that can inspire others to do the same. This can lead to a workplace where cooperation, collaboration and mutual respect are the norm. Kindness is a powerful weapon for professional success. By using it in the way described, you can help build positive relationships, solve challenges effectively, and create a healthy and productive workplace. Kindness is a resource that should be cultivated and practiced by anyone seeking to succeed in their career.

- Recognition and Appreciation: Recognizing the good work of colleagues is an act of generosity that has a significant impact on morale and workplace relationships. A sincere "Thank you for your help" may seem like a simple gesture, but it has the power to make colleagues feel appreciated and valued. Gratitude is a form of recognition that can elevate people's mood and promote a culture of collaboration and mutual support. Showing appreciation not only strengthens relationships but can also motivate colleagues to give their best. Knowing that one's work is noticed and appreciated creates a sense of personal accomplishment and satisfaction, which in turn can translate into deeper commitment and greater dedication to work. In addition, sincere appreciation contributes to a climate of mutual trust and respect among colleagues. When people feel appreciated, they are more likely to collaborate positively, share ideas and support each other in times of challenge. Recognizing the good work of colleagues through sincere appreciation is a powerful gesture that improves the work climate, strengthens relationships and promotes a positive workplace. Do not underestimate the importance of expressing gratitude and acknowledging the contributions of others; this simple act can make all the difference in creating a cohesive and motivated team.

- Improve Communication: Addressing conflicts and misunderstandings in an open and constructive way is essential to promoting a healthy workplace and to resolving complex situations effectively. Open communication allows problems to be addressed head-on, rather than avoiding or ignoring tensions that can undermine workplace relationships. Frank and respectful discussion is a valuable tool for conflict resolution. When those involved can express their opinions and concerns in a civil and respectful manner, a space is created in which an optimal solution can be sought. In this context, comparing different perspectives can lead to new insights and interesting ideas for improving the workplace. Maintaining a calm and relaxed atmosphere during discussion is equally important. A tense or aggressive environment can hinder communication and make conflict resolution more difficult. In contrast, a climate in which people feel heard and respected promotes more productive and constructive discussion. Addressing conflicts in an open and constructive manner, maintaining a respectful tone and promoting a calm climate, is crucial to resolving problems in the workplace and contributing to a more harmonious and productive workplace.

Empathic communication

Empathy is a secret ingredient for building lasting relationships. It means being able to understand and share the feelings of others.

Here's how you can apply empathy in your professional relationships:

- <u>Seek to Understand</u>: Understanding others is a crucial skill in a professional setting. When a colleague or superior faces a problem or a concern, it is crucial to try to understand their perspective and show genuine interest in what they are experiencing. This skill of listening and understanding can foster effective communication, improve workplace relationships, and contribute to the overall success of the organization. A key element in understanding others is the skill of putting yourself in their shoes. It means lining up your perspective with theirs, trying to see the situation from their angle. This requires empathy, the skill of recognizing and sharing the emotions of others. When a colleague or superior has a problem, it is essential to avoid hasty judgments or immediate criticism. Instead, take a moment to consider how they might feel and how that situation might affect their experience. Understanding is an essential skill in a professional setting. Seeking to understand the perspective of others, asking open-ended questions, practicing active listening and showing genuine interest can improve relationships, promote effective communication and contribute to the overall success of the organization. In a working world where collaboration and mutual understanding are critical, the skill of understanding others is a valuable resource that can make all the difference in your professional success. When a colleague or superior has a problem or concern, try to understand their perspective. Don't think as if the problem is yours but try to put yourself in their shoes; only then can you understand their frustration. Ask open-ended questions to encourage discussion and show interest in what they are going through. To truly understand others, it is important to create a space where they can express themselves freely. Using open questions is an effective technique to encourage discussion and gain a deeper understanding of the situation. Open-ended questions require detailed answers and are not limited to a simple "yes" or "no." For example, instead of asking "Do you have a problem?" you might ask "Can you tell me more about the situation you are facing?"

- <u>Share Your Experiences</u>: Sharing personal experiences can be a powerful way to make meaningful connections and help colleagues feel less alone in the challenges they face. When a colleague is experiencing a similar situation to one you have overcome before, sharing your experience can create an empathetic bond. For example, you can start by saying, "I know what you mean. When I went through a similar situation, I did this..." or "I know what you're going through. I, like you, had a similar experience. Then I did this...." This shows that you understand their concerns and are willing to share your knowledge and coping strategies. This sharing of personal experiences creates a sense of solidarity and support among colleagues. Your colleague knows that he or she is not the only one experiencing this challenge and feels less isolated. This connection can strengthen professional bonds and create a workplace where people feel more comfortable asking for help or sharing their challenges. Sharing personal experiences can be a way to create deeper connections in the workplace and help colleagues overcome difficulties together. This helps build a corporate culture based on collaboration and mutual support.

- Offer Support: Offering your support in a genuine way to someone who's going through a difficult time is an extraordinarily powerful act of compassion. When you see that someone is struggling, you can address them with words such as, "I'm here for you if you need to talk or if there is anything I can help you with," or "We know what you are going through and we want you to know that if you need help, we are there." This act of kindness and compassion can significantly impact people's lives. It provides them with a sense of support and solidarity at a time when they may feel alone or overwhelmed. This can give them strength to face challenges and hope for a better future. In addition, the gesture of extending a hand to others reflects the power of empathy and human kindness in improving the lives of others. It shows that you genuinely care about the well-being of others and are willing to offer your help without expecting anything in return. Offer your support in an authentic and powerful way to connect with others, ease their emotional burden, and spread kindness in the workplace. It can help create an atmosphere of mutual support and improve people's quality of life.

- Listen Actively: Active listening is another key element. It means paying attention to what the other person is saying, without interruptions or premature judgments.

Make conscious efforts to listen not only to the words, but also to the tone of voice, body language, and underlying emotions. This kind of listening can help you pick up important nuances and details that might otherwise be overlooked. This means not only passively listening, but also asking probing questions to show that you genuinely care about their situation. Ask how they feel about the situation, what challenges they are experiencing, and if there are ways you could help. A crucial part of understanding is showing genuine interest in what the other person is facing. Genuine interest can also be evidenced through body language and facial expressions. Maintaining eye contact, smiling when appropriate, and nodding to show that you are following the conversation are signs that will communicate your empathy.

At the beginning of my employment as an executive assistant at my hometown hospital, I had a reputation for being very professional but also somewhat distant and cold. That changed when I decided to develop the skill of communicating empathically.

The turning point came during a leadership and communication seminar that I had decided to attend of my own free will. During one of the sessions, I realized how important empathy was in professional relationships. I realized that it was not only about completing tasks efficiently, but also about understanding the needs and emotions of others.

To begin my journey of developing empathy, I began to pay attention to details in conversations. Instead of just giving quick, pragmatic answers, I began to listen carefully to the concerns and feelings of my interlocutors. I asked open-ended questions to better understand their perspectives.

One of the first challenges I faced was with my Director. Usually, interactions with him were simple and formal. However, I decided to change my approach. During one meeting, when my Director seemed concerned, instead of just focusing on the agenda, I asked politely, "Is everything okay, Director? What's bothering you."

My Director was surprised by this attention and opened up to me about a challenge he was facing. I listened without judgment and offered my support. From that moment, our professional relationship changed. My Director began to involve me more in projects and to appreciate my contribution not only as an assistant but also as a confidant.

I applied the same empathy with colleagues as well. Instead of just sending aseptic e-mails, I started writing more personal messages and trying to understand how my colleagues felt about different projects. My empathy made me a key resource on the team, able to mediate discussions and find solutions that took everyone's needs into account.

But the real test of my new skill came when my colleague, Michelle, was going through a difficult time in her personal life. I not only listened to Michelle's concerns but also offered practical support, enabling her to manage work more flexibly during that difficult time.

This is part of my professional story but a clear example of how empathy can improve professional relationships. People were turning to me for advice and support, and my positive influence spread throughout the entire workplace.

Ultimately, I had learned that empathic communication not only made interactions more meaningful, but also had a tangible impact on my career. I realized that being empathetic did not mean being weak, but could be a driving force in achieving professional goals and building strong relationships. I had put into practice a valuable lesson: true professional success is not only based on technical skills, but also on the ability to connect with others in an authentic and compassionate way.

Cultivating effective interpersonal relationships takes time and effort, but it is worth the effort. When you have positive relationships with those you work with, the flow of communication is smoother, projects proceed better, and the workplace becomes more enjoyable. Your ability to communicate with empathy will help create a harmonious workplace and make you emerge as an outstanding executive assistant.

Chapter 2

Organization and Time Management

Being a successful executive assistant requires more than just communication skills. You must have complete control over time management and organization to be truly effective in your role. In this section, we will explore in depth the principles and strategies for mastering the art of time management and organization.

Planning and Organization

Planning is fundamental to effective time management. Start your day or week with a clear and well-organized task list. You can adopt a system that best suits your work style, such as a simple list written in your planner or using a task management application.

A practical example of scheduling might be as follows: imagine that your supervisor has assigned you three main tasks for the day. Take a moment in the morning to break these tasks down into specific actions and set deadlines for each. For example, if one of the main tasks is to prepare a presentation, list the necessary steps, such as research, slide creation, and final review, assigning each an approximate time to complete it.

This division of tasks will help you maintain control over your day and avoid feeling overwhelmed. It will also allow you to focus on specific tasks in a more focused way and better estimate how much time each task will take. A well-organized task list also allows you to prioritize more clearly, so you can focus on the most important and urgent tasks first. This way you can optimize your time and maximize productivity.

Planning is a key element in managing your time effectively. Organizing tasks into specific actions and setting deadlines will help you maintain control over your day and work more efficiently. Planning allows you to set clear priorities and focus on what is really important to your professional success....

Priorities and Delegation

Not all tasks are equally important. Learn to identify urgent and important tasks, and give them the proper priority. Use the principle of the Eisenhower Matrix, which divides tasks into four categories: urgent and important, important but not urgent, urgent but not important, and not urgent and not important. Focus your time and energy on the urgent and important activities, but do not neglect the important but not urgent ones, because they are often the keys to long-term success.

Here is a concrete example: suppose you have received an urgent request from a client and, at the same time, need to prepare an important presentation for a meeting the following week. In this case, the client's request is urgent but the presentation is important. Take the time to satisfy the client, but do not neglect the preparation of the presentation by planning it in advance.

Don't try to do everything yourself. Learn to delegate appropriate tasks to colleagues or team members. Delegation frees up your time to focus on more valuable activities.

Managing Interruptions.

Interruptions are a common factor that can undermine your productivity, but there are strategies for successfully managing them. For example, if your colleagues tend to call you frequently for questions or assistance, you might consider setting specific times when you are available to respond to their requests. This allows you to focus on your tasks without constant interruptions.

An additional suggestion is to adopt the Tomato technique. This method involves working intensely for a predetermined period of time, often 25 minutes, followed by a short break. This cycle of work and break helps maintain high concentration and increase productivity. During the 25 minutes of concentrated work, you can ignore other distractions and focus fully on the task at hand. Once the cycle is complete, take a short break to rest your mind before tackling the next work cycle.

Managing interruptions is essential to maintaining productivity and focus. These tips can help you limit unwanted interruptions and improve your work efficiency.

Office Organization

Office organization is essential for you because it helps you perform your role efficiently and effectively. A well-organized office means having everything you need easily accessible, reducing the time spent searching for documents or information. This allows you to handle requests and deadlines in a timely manner, positively impressing your superiors and colleagues.

Good organization also promotes greater productivity and reduces stress, as you feel more in control of your activities. In addition, a neat and organized workplace helps convey a professional image and positively affects your reputation. Investing time in office organization is an investment in your professional success.

Make sure your space is perfectly organized, with everything you need at your fingertips.

Keep important documents in well-labeled files, use a clean desk, and create an effective filing system. Learn to get rid of unnecessary items and paper that can create clutter.

For example, set aside time each week to clean up your desk and file important documents. Use folders or binders to organize your documents so they are easily accessible when you need them.

Use an electronic calendar or paper agenda to keep track of all important deadlines. Be sure to set reminders so that you are notified in advance.

Just as every chef has his or her own set of knives, every self-respecting executive assistant has his or her own agenda and pen.

Continuous Monitoring and Improvement

Periodically, assess how much you have achieved against your goals. This allows you to make adjustments to your planning and improve your efficiency over time. Assessing progress is essential to understand how far you have come and what you still need to do, if you are behind schedule what to do to catch up, and if you are ahead of schedule how you can better optimize the resources we have available.

Invest in your personal and professional growth. Attend training courses, read books on personal effectiveness, and always look for ways to improve your organization and time management skills. In life, you never stop learning.

Time management is a skill that requires constant practice, but once mastered, it will enable you to successfully meet daily challenges and maintain a balance between work and personal life. With careful planning, effective organization, and thoughtful time management, you will be able to maximize your productivity, reduce stress, and maintain a high level of professionalism in your work. Read on and find out how to become an outstanding executive assistant!

Chapter 3

Mastery in Technology

In the modern world, technology has become an indispensable ally for success in any field of work. In this chapter, we will explore how you can become a true expert in using the most useful applications and software to increase your productivity and simplify your office work.

Advanced Office Tools

The Microsoft Office suite is one of the most widely used software tools in the office. You will need to master Word for creating professional documents, Excel for managing data and tables, and PowerPoint for creating impactful presentations. There are other software programs out there that perform the same tasks, but in my personal opinion these software programs and those that will be named below are the most comprehensive for your secretarial work.

Google's G Suite: You will also use the powerful applications offered by Google, such as Gmail,

Google Calendar, Google Docs, Sheets, and Slides. These cloud-based tools make it easy for you to collaborate with colleagues and superiors and also allow you to work from home should you need to.

Electronic Document Management.

Learn how to use electronic document storage and management systems, such as SharePoint or Google Drive. These tools make it easy to share, access and search documents.

Learn how to use electronic signature services such as Adobe Sign or DocuSign to speed up the document signing process, reducing the need to print and scan, thus saving time and paper.

Automating Tasks.

Explore automation software for repetitive processes such as Zapier or Microsoft Power Automate to simplify repetitive tasks. For example, you can automate sending confirmation emails or updating data in spreadsheets.

Familiarize yourself with the use of virtual assistants such as Apple's Siri or Google Assistant to simplify tasks such as scheduling meetings or quickly searching for information.

IT Security.

Learn best practices for cyber security. This includes password management, identifying phishing emails, and using antivirus and security tools.

Understand how to protect sensitive company data and confidential documents. Learn how to make regular backups and manage file access permissions carefully.

Continuous Learning

Invest time in continuing technical education. Participate in online or offline courses to improve your skills in specific software and stay up-to-date on the latest technology.

Don't be afraid to explore new tools and applications. Technology is constantly evolving, and being open to innovation will allow you to remain competitive.

Continuous IT learning is crucial for an executive assistant because advanced digital skills improve efficiency in managing documents, e-mails and business software. This enables faster and more effective communication, reduces errors, and increases overall office productivity. In addition, knowledge of new technologies and updated software keeps the executive assistant abreast of the evolving needs of the modern work environment, making her more adaptable and valuable to the organization. In an increasingly digitized world, continuous IT learning is essential to ensure that an executive assistant can perform her duties effectively and competitively.

My second best skill is computer literacy, which is a great advantage in this field as it has become essential in many professions, including that of executive assistant. However, it is important to point out that not everyone may already possess complete expertise in this field, which is why I recommend that you seek in-depth training.

For those who are already working as executive assistants or aspire to become one, investing in IT training is a wise step. Modern administrative offices rely heavily on software to manage data, documents and communications, and possessing solid IT skills can make you emerge as a highly efficient and competent professional.

The recommendation to seek out an accredited facility for a comprehensive course on the most widely used software packages in offices is very pertinent. The importance of these courses lies in the fact that they should culminate with a follow-up exam.

The final exam is essential because it objectively demonstrates that you have acquired the skills necessary to use the software effectively. In addition, the issuance of a diploma or certificate of proficiency is an official attestation of your level of proficiency, which can be a significant value-add to your resume. Employers value accredited training and certificates that demonstrate your skills.

Avoid those courses that only give a certificate of attendance and have no final exam to pass. A certificate of attendance only indicates that you have attended the course but not necessarily that you have learned or mastered the necessary skills. These certificates have little professional relevance and may not make a difference in the job market.

Computer knowledge is a valuable skill for executive assistants. Comprehensive, accredited training in the most widely used software is highly recommended and should culminate in an exam resulting in a diploma or certificate. This investment in your IT training can open doors and greatly enhance your career prospects. It is an important step in distinguishing yourself in the executive assistant profession.

With mastery in technology, you will become a valuable executive assistant for your company. Your skill in using digital tools will enable you to perform tasks more efficiently, collaborate more effectively, and manage data more securely. Technology is a very powerful ally for success, and learning how to make the most of it is a smart choice for your professional future.

Chapter 4

Problem Solving and Decision Making

A successful executive assistant is more than just a task performer. He or she is a key figure in problem solving and decision making. In this chapter, I will guide you through the tools and strategies you need to approach difficult situations with confidence and determination.

Problem Analysis.

Learn to clearly recognize what the problem is. This may require information gathering, interviews, or consulting resources.

Once the problem is identified, try to discover its root causes. This may involve investigating processes, evaluating data or analyzing relationships among various factors.

Recognizing a problem and uncovering its root cause is critical for an executive assistant because it enables her to deal with challenges effectively and make focused, effective decisions.

This skill enables you to quickly resolve operational issues, improve internal processes and communications, and anticipate potential future problems. In addition, by identifying underlying causes, you can help prevent recurrences, increasing the efficiency and productivity of your office.

The ability to address problems competently and proactively is a crucial attribute for ensuring efficient workflow and maintaining a harmonious work environment.

Problem Solving Strategies.

Bring a team together or have a one-on-one brainstorming session to generate problem-solving ideas. This creative process can lead to innovative solutions.

Do you know this saying. "If two eyes see better than one, two minds think more than one."

By collaborating and sharing views, better results can be achieved, more creative solutions to problems can be found, and more informed decisions can be made. Brainstorming brings out the value of diversity of thought and cooperation in solving challenges and achieving common goals.

Once you have gathered several solutions, learn to evaluate and rank them according to their potential effectiveness. This will enable you to focus your efforts on the most promising solutions and thus avoid wasting energy and resources.

Test the identified solutions and monitor the results. This step will allow you to determine whether a solution is working or whether changes need to be made.

Effective Decision Making.

Effective decision making requires a number of crucial steps. First, it is critical to gather all relevant information. This may include data, expert opinions, or feedback from others involved. Comprehensive information gathering gives you a solid foundation on which to base your decision.

Next, it is important to consider several possible options for dealing with the situation. A useful approach is to list all available alternatives without excluding any. This allows you to explore a full range of possibilities and weigh the pros and cons of each.

Finally, you need to assess the time available to you to make a decision. Some situations may require an immediate response, while others allow you to take more time. However, it is crucial to avoid wasting time unnecessarily, as delay could lead to problems and missed deadlines. Therefore, it is important to strike a balance between gathering in-depth information and meeting the timelines necessary to make an informed and timely decision.

Effective decision making involves gathering comprehensive information, exploring different options, and evaluating the time available. These steps help you make informed decisions and manage situations efficiently.

Communication and Implementation

Effective communication of decisions is critical to ensure that everyone is aligned and understanding about what has been decided and why. After making a decision, it is important to communicate it clearly and concisely to all stakeholders, taking into account the audience and using appropriate language for the specific audience. Make sure everyone understands the reason behind the decision and the actions needed to implement it. This prevents misunderstandings and future conflicts.

Once the decision is implemented, it is essential to monitor the results. This step is crucial because it allows you to assess whether the decision is having the desired effects. If you notice that things are not going as planned or that there are unforeseen obstacles, be prepared to revise your decision and make changes if necessary. Flexibility in considering new information or changes in the situation is an important quality for good leadership and for ensuring the success of decisions made.

Clearly communicating decisions and carefully monitoring results are critical steps in decision making. These help maintain alignment and effectiveness in achieving the goals set by the decision, and allow you to proactively adapt to any changes or challenges that may arise.

Continuous Learning

After solving a problem or making a decision, take time to reflect on the experience; this is a crucial step in your professional development. This reflection allows you to learn from the situation and improve your decision-making skills.

First, it is important to ask yourself what you learned from the situation. Did you gain new knowledge or skills? Did you improve your understanding of organizational dynamics or interpersonal relationships? These learnings can be valuable for your professional development.

Second, you should consider whether you could have handled the situation better. Were there errors or omissions that you could avoid in the future? This constructive self-criticism helps you identify areas where you can improve. It is also essential to consider whether there are resources or alternatives that you did not consider during the decision-making process. This reflection can lead to a more comprehensive view of the options available in similar situations.

Reflecting on how you might better handle similar situations in the future helps you develop a more effective strategy for dealing with similar challenges. This may include applying new skills or taking a different approach.

Investing in your professional growth by attending courses or seminars on problem management and decision making is an important step. These learning opportunities help you develop more advanced skills and stay current on best practices in the field of problem management and decision making.

Dealing with problems and making decisions are an integral part of an executive assistant's role. With the right skills and strategies, you will be able to face any challenge with confidence and contribute positively to the company's success. Remember that every problem is a learning opportunity, and every decision made wisely can lead to extraordinary results.

Chapter 5

Managing Stress and Maintaining a Work-Life Balance

The job of executive assistant can be extremely rewarding, but also very demanding. To perform your role to the best of your ability and maintain a high level of productivity, it is essential to learn how to manage stress and maintain a healthy work-life balance. In this chapter, we will explore strategies and techniques for dealing with stress and fully enjoying your life outside the office.

Understanding Stress

The first step in managing stress is to recognize the sources that generate it. Stressors for an executive assistant can vary depending on the work environment, specific responsibilities, and the personality of the person involved. However, there are some common sources of stress that often affect professionals in this position.

Some of the main stressors for an executive assistant can be high workload, deadlines and time pressure, stressful work environment, frequent changes in priorities, lack of time management, financial responsibilities, multitasking role, technology-related stress, and Lack of recognition.

Take note of specific situations that put you under pressure.

Learn to recognize the effects of stress on your physical and mental health. Chronic stress can lead to problems such as anxiety, insomnia, and physical health problems. Awareness is the first step in addressing the problem.

It is important to note that stress management is essential to an executive assistant's well-being. This may include strategies such as organizing time, communicating effectively with superiors, delegating tasks when possible, and seeking support from colleagues when needed.

Stress Management Techniques.

- Mindfulness Practice.

Mindfulness is a practice that has roots in the ancient Buddhist tradition but has been adapted and integrated into many cultures and contexts, including Western psychology. It is an approach to life and self-awareness that involves deep attention to and awareness of one's thoughts, emotions, physical sensations, and surroundings.

The practice of mindfulness can contribute to improved interpersonal relationships, reduced stress, and increased psychological well-being. Many people use it as a tool to manage anxiety, depression and other psychological conditions. It can help develop greater empathy and understanding toward others.

You will learn how to practice mindfulness through meditation, mindful breathing and paying attention to your thoughts and feelings.

A popular book on mindfulness is "The Miracle of Mindfulness" by Thich Nhat Hanh. Thich Nhat Hanh is a Vietnamese Buddhist monk and a well-known mindfulness teacher.

"The Miracle of Mindfulness" is a recommended read for anyone interested in exploring mindfulness, whether a beginner or someone more experienced in the practice.

- Regular physical activity is an effective way to reduce stress.

Do you know the saying, "Mens sana in corpore sano"? It is a famous Latin saying that means "healthy mind in a healthy body." This phrase emphasizes the importance of maintaining a balance between physical and mental health.

It means that you are more likely to have a healthy and clear mind in a body that receives proper care through a healthy diet, exercise and sufficient sleep. This philosophy promotes the concept that mental and physical well-being are interconnected and mutually influential. By maintaining a healthy body, you can support a clear and positive mind, and vice versa, promoting a balanced and fulfilling life in both your personal and work spheres.

Find an activity you enjoy, whether swimming, yoga, running or dancing, and incorporate it into your weekly routine.

- Time management is a crucial skill for reducing stress.

We have already talked about how time management is a necessary skill for getting your work done, but it is equally important for reducing stress.

When we organize our activities effectively, we are able to deal with them in a calmer and more productive way. First, planning allows us to prioritize and devote time to the most important activities, reducing the sense of overload. In addition, effective organization helps avoid the very last minute, which can be a source of stress.

A well-structured agenda also provides space for rest and recharging, reducing the buildup of tension. In addition, time management can improve productivity by freeing up more time for relaxation.

Finally, proper planning allows you to take time to deal with problems or decisions, avoiding rushed decisions that can cause additional stress. Overall, time management helps create a more balanced and controlled routine, greatly reducing stress levels in the personal and professional spheres.

Creating a Work-Personal Life Balance.

Setting limits is crucial for an executive assistant to create a balance between work and personal life. First, boundaries help prevent burnout by protecting mental and physical health.

This profession can be intensely demanding, so establishing clear work schedules prevents work from overly encroaching on personal life. In addition, having clear boundaries promotes productivity.

Learn to say "no" when necessary and set clear boundaries between work and personal life. This will allow you to set aside the necessary time for rest and relaxation.

When an executive assistant is well rested and has time to herself, she will be more efficient and focused during working hours. Finally, setting boundaries allows you to nurture personal relationships, take care of yourself, and pursue hobbies and passions, thus contributing to a balanced and satisfying life outside the work environment.

Devote quality time to your personal life. Plan special times with family and friends, and do activities you are passionate about outside the work environment.

In a demanding role such as executive assistant, the professional demands can be intense and stressful. Without proper balance, you risk burning out and experiencing increased stress and fatigue. Investing time in your personal life will allow you to recharge your energy, improve mental and physical health, and prevent the onset of job dissatisfaction. It also fosters stronger and more fulfilling relationships with family and friends.

A balance between work and personal life not only increases happiness and productivity, but also helps to preserve long-term health and support a successful career in the long run.

Continuous Learning.

Attend courses or workshops on stress management. These sessions can offer you new strategies for dealing with stressful situations more effectively.

Seek out resources, books, and expert advice on creating and maintaining a healthy work-life balance. Continuous learning will help you develop a resilient mindset.

Managing stress and maintaining a balance between work and personal life are critical skills for preserving your long-term health and happiness. Remember that taking care of yourself is essential to performing your role as an executive assistant successfully. With the right techniques and consistent commitment, you will be able to face work challenges calmly and enjoy your life outside the office in a satisfying way.

Chapter 6

Professional Growth and Continuing Development

Since you are a very attentive reader you will certainly have noticed how at the end of each chapter I advised you to spend time and resources on your education, this is because your career as an executive assistant is an ever-evolving journey, one that requires adaptability and constant growth.

Professional growth and ongoing development are vital for an executive assistant. Imagine your career as a long and compelling journey, where each stop represents an opportunity to acquire new skills that will enable you to excel in your role and contribute meaningfully to the organization in which you work.

First, the world of work is constantly evolving, with new technologies, processes and trends emerging regularly. Keeping your skills up-to-date is critical to staying relevant and competitive. Constantly learning new computer tools, software and applications allows you to work more efficiently and meet the growing demands of the modern secretary's office.

Continuing education also gives you the opportunity to advance your career. You can aspire to more responsible roles, such as coordinators or office managers, but these positions usually require a wide range of skills, including leadership and time management. By investing in your professional growth, you will be better prepared for such challenges.

In addition, networking is a key element in your professional growth. Attending industry events, conferences, and networking groups allows you to make connections with colleagues and experienced professionals. These connections can lead to job opportunities, consulting and mentorship, which can accelerate your growth and guide you along your professional path.

In addition to technical skills, develop soft skills such as effective communication, empathy, and stress management, which are critical for success in your profession.

In addition, soft skill development is necessary for an executive assistant because it fosters effective communication with colleagues and superiors, increases empathy when interacting with clients and colleagues, and helps manage stress in complex situations. These skills, such as active listening skills and relationship management, are crucial to professional success and to creating a harmonious and productive work environment.

Self-confidence is another important aspect. When you invest in your continuous development, you gain more confidence in your abilities. You know that you are prepared to meet challenges, and this confidence is reflected in your work performance and in your interactions with colleagues and superiors.

Finally, professional growth can lead to greater job satisfaction and achievement of your career goals. It gives you a sense of personal accomplishment and helps you feel valued and motivated in your role as an executive assistant.

In conclusion, professional growth and ongoing development are essential for an executive assistant, as they enable you to stay abreast of a constantly changing world of work, advance your career, and build a future of success and job satisfaction. Invest in yourself and embrace learning opportunities because they are the key to a bright future in your profession.

Chapter 7

The Business Card

Appearance as a business card is a fundamental principle of personal presentation and nonverbal communication. This means that your image-the way you dress, take care of your personal hygiene, and present yourself physically-plays a significant role in impressing others and communicating who you are and what you stand for.

When you take care of your appearance, you demonstrate attention to detail and respect for yourself and others. Appropriate and well-groomed clothing can convey professionalism, confidence, and respect for the work environment or occasion. Conversely, a neglected or poorly groomed appearance can send negative signals, such as disinterest or lack of attention.

Personal appearance is a crucial aspect for an executive assistant working in a company, as it represents the company's calling card as well as itself. How you present yourself physically greatly affects how others perceive you and can have a significant impact on your career. That is why it is important to take care of your appearance:

Personal appearance is certainly an important element in forming a first impression, but it goes beyond clothing. It involves a complex set of factors including posture, body language, facial expression, and personal grooming. These elements communicate valuable information about individuals and can greatly influence the perception of others.

For example, an upright posture can convey security and confidence, while a hunched posture can suggest insecurity. A genuine smile can make others feel at ease and help create a positive atmosphere. A firm handshake can indicate determination and assertiveness.

However, it is important to remember that appearance is only one part of a person's overall identity. Actions, behavior, and skills play an equally significant role in shaping an image of success and credibility. You may look impeccable, but if your behavior is unprofessional or your skills are not up to par, your image may be compromised.

Therefore, it is critical to balance attention to appearance with developing your professional skills and maintaining ethical and respectful behavior. A complete and consistent presentation of yourself, including both appearance and behavior, will help you build a reputation for success and credibility in the professional world. In conclusion, while appearance plays an important role, it is only one of many elements that contribute to a person's overall image in the work environment.

Here are some tips in this regard for having an image of success and credibility.

- Attire that is clean, well groomed and appropriate for the business environment conveys a sense of professionalism. This is especially important because you are often the first person customers, suppliers and colleagues come into contact with.

- A neat appearance suggests reliability and attention to detail, attributes that are essential for an executive assistant. Your personal presentation can influence the confidence others have in your ability to handle important responsibilities and information.

- Matching your appearance to the company's dress code and values is essential. Adhere to company guidelines so you help create a sense of belonging and consistency within the organization.

- Your appearance communicates many things to others, even without speaking. Your posture, personal grooming, and the way you dress can influence others' perceptions of your confidence, competence, and authority.

- Often, first impressions are hard to change. So be sure to make a positive first impression through a polished and professional appearance.

- Showing care for your appearance can indicate a respect for your work and those you work with. Show that you take your role seriously and understand the importance of your position in the company.

- Smile. Smiling reflects positively on your professional image. It communicates optimism, confidence and a positive mindset, attributes valued in a work setting. A genuine smile creates a friendly and welcoming atmosphere and can make people feel at ease and promotes a positive work climate.

So back straight, chest out, take care of your body, dress neatly and appropriately for the workplace, be polite, and above all, never forget to smile.

In summary, personal appearance is your calling card as an executive assistant, and it can greatly influence your reputation and how others perceive your competence and reliability. Therefore, paying attention to how you present yourself physically is a key element for success in your career.

Chapter 8

Love your job

The importance of loving your job is a key aspect in both the professional sphere and in your personal life. First, it is important to recognize that attitude, willingness and disposition to take risks are key elements in creating a positive bond with both job and one's profession. This bond is not primarily influenced by external factors, but is more a matter of individual predisposition and how one approaches job.

Love of job is a powerful motivational force. When an individual loves what he or she does, he or she is more inclined to engage fully and constantly strive for excellence. Enthusiasm and passion for one's responsibilities result in deeper commitment and greater dedication to providing high-quality services. This positive attitude not only improves overall performance, but also helps solidify the perception of one's value within the organization.

Love of job acts as an intrinsic source of motivation. When a person finds meaning and satisfaction in their tasks, they are more likely to remain consistently motivated and focused. A motivated executive assistant is able to meet challenges with determination, maintain high levels of productivity, and successfully manage the increasing demands of his or her role.

Those who enjoy their job are usually inclined to seek opportunities for professional growth and development. This desire for continuous learning makes the individual more versatile and able to tackle a wide range of tasks, thus opening the door to new career opportunities.

An executive assistant who loves his or her job is also able to develop more effective working relationships. His or her passion and dedication can have a positive impact on group dynamics and communication with colleagues and superiors. A person who is passionate about job is generally more pleasant to work with, creating a more harmonious work environment.

Love for one's job drives one to invest time and energy to perform it to the best of one's ability. This leads to less risk of procrastination or superficial execution of tasks. Enthusiasm leads to greater efficiency, saving valuable time and avoiding burnout caused by overwork.

In addition, love of job stimulates innovation and creativity. A passionate executive assistant is more likely to seek new approaches to challenges and come up with creative solutions to problems. This mindset can lead to significant improvements in the company's processes and operations.

It should also be emphasized that love for one's job has a positive impact on overall health. When one is able to combine the verb "to work" with the verb "to love," the individual benefits in terms of energy, creativity, reliability, quality of work, and the ability to successfully deal with the inevitable difficulties that every job entails. Love for job gives one an extra edge and helps one better handle the challenges and difficulties that any type of employment inevitably poses. Being passionate about job instills strength, courage and boosts self-esteem, fueling the desire to improve and take care of oneself and others. Ultimately, love for one's job is a powerful catalyst for professional and personal success.

Loving one's job as an executive assistant is a key aspect of achieving professional success and satisfaction. But how do you love your job?

1. Distinguish positive from negative aspects: it is important to recognize that no job is perfect. Identify the positive facets of your role and show sincere gratitude for them. At the same time, try to separate the negative aspects and consider whether you can gradually change them or strengthen the positive ones.

2. Avoid prejudices: keep an open mind with respect to your employment and the context in which you operate. Often, prejudices can limit your ability to fully appreciate your work.

3. Don't personalize: when you face difficult situations or receive critical feedback, try not to take everything personally. Focus on solutions and improvement instead of feeling attacked.

4. Be optimistic: optimism is a key element in developing a love for job. Keep a positive outlook even when facing challenges or difficult times.

5. Constantly nurture your love for job, it requires daily care: set goals and challenges for

yourself. Try to gain new experiences and constantly improve.

6. Accept challenges as opportunities: difficulties are an integral part of any job. See challenges as opportunities to grow and surpass yourself instead of avoiding them.

7. Overcome difficulties: love for job will give you the strength to overcome difficult times. Don't let obstacles bring you down, but face them with determination.

8. Embrace every difficulty as an opportunity to improve yourself: every obstacle can be a stepping stone to higher levels of professional competence and satisfaction.

In conclusion, love of job is a crucial element of a successful executive assistant. A passion for one's responsibilities can increase motivation, improve performance, and open doors to opportunities for growth. An executive assistant who loves his or her job and cares about its well-being is able to pursue a satisfying and successful long-term career.

Chapter 9

Multitasking

You have no doubt been tasked with handling a wide range of tasks and responsibilities simultaneously. In this case, the ability to work in multitasking is vital. Multitasking is the ability to successfully manage and complete multiple tasks simultaneously, and for an executive assistant, this skill is critical to being effective and productive.

One of the key elements that makes multitasking so crucial for an executive assistant is the wide range of tasks they face on a daily basis. From communicating with clients and colleagues to managing deadlines, from scheduling meetings to managing documents, there are many different tasks that require simultaneous attention. Without the ability to handle multiple tasks, it may be difficult for an executive assistant to deal with the volume of work effectively.

The multitasking can lead to a significant increase in efficiency and productivity. While working on one thing, it is possible to start a second task that requires less concentration. For example, while waiting for a response to an e-mail, you can devote time to organizing documentation. This type of approach makes better use of time and allows you to complete more tasks in a shorter period.

The multitasking is an essential tool for time management. Executive assistants often have to meet tight deadlines and plan their days carefully. Multitasking allows them to effectively spread their work over multiple tasks and avoid wasting time. This is especially important when facing sudden changes in priorities or emergencies.

The business environment can be dynamic and changing. Priorities can change rapidly, and an executive assistant must be able to adapt with agility to these changes. Multitasking allows for seamless transition from one task to another and prompt response to new needs or requests.

Managing communications is a key part of an executive assistant's role. This includes not only sending and receiving e-mail, but also managing phone calls, attending meetings, and coordinating communications among team members. Multitasking is essential to effectively manage all these activities without losing sight of any important communication.

Techniques for mastering multitasking

Now that we understand the importance of multitasking for an executive assistant, let's look at some techniques for developing and mastering this skill:

1.   The first key to effective multitasking is to set priorities. Identify the most urgent and important tasks and focus on them. Use tools such as task lists and calendars to keep track of tasks and organize your days.

2.   Break down complex tasks into smaller, more manageable steps. This makes it easier to focus on one aspect at a time without being overwhelmed by the complexity of the entire task.

3.   Organize your day into blocks of work dedicated to specific tasks. For example, devote one block of time to email management, another to meeting planning, and so on. This allows you to focus on one type of task at a time.

4.   Take advantage of technology tools such as task management apps and digital calendars to keep track of tasks and deadlines. These tools can simplify task planning and management.

5.   Multitasking is a skill that can be honed over time. Constantly practice switching between tasks and learn from your mistakes. Over time, you will become more efficient at performing multiple tasks simultaneously.

6.   Minimize distractions while working. Turn off non-essential notifications on your computer and phone and create a quiet, focused work environment.

7.   Maintain good physical and mental health. Work-life balance, a balanced diet, exercise and rest are all important to maintain the energy and focus needed for multitasking.

In conclusion, multitasking is a crucial skill for an executive assistant. To be effective in a complex and dynamic work environment, it is critical to be able to handle multiple tasks simultaneously. Using prioritization, organization, and time management techniques, you can master multitasking and become a more productive and efficient professional.

Chapter 10

The Art of Frosting

Imagine being in a bakery and looking at a display case of delicious pastries. There are muffins, cakes, and cookies, all impeccably and tantalizingly decorated. However, there is one particular cake that catches your attention in a special way: it is a cake with a shiny, glossy frosting that almost seems to dance in the light. It is as if this cake has something extra, a touch of magic that sets it apart from other cakes. In a work context, putting "frosting" in your work means adding that extra something that sets you apart from others and makes you stand out for excellence.

Putting frosting in your work is a powerful and universal concept that applies to any professional field. Regardless of your industry, always striving to stand out with excellence is a key to success.

In a world where competition is fierce, standing out is essential. Frosting allows you to stand out in a sea of competitors. It makes your contribution unique and valuable.

When you add that extra touch to your work, you leave a lasting impression. Your colleagues, superiors or clients will remember your dedication to excellence and be more likely to trust you and seek you out for future collaborations. Putting icing on your work is rewarding on a personal level. It gives you a feeling of accomplishment and satisfaction that goes beyond the task at hand. This personal motivation can fuel your passion and determination.

When you put frosting on you increase your credibility and gain the trust of people who interact with you. Whether you are a self-employed professional looking for clients, an employee seeking a promotion, or an entrepreneur looking for investors, credibility is key.

It often means, too, being innovative. You are constantly looking for better ways to do things, to solve problems, and to meet the needs of your clients or employer.

Personal satisfaction is a direct result of putting icing in your work. When you have the confidence that you have given your all and exceeded expectations, you feel great satisfaction in knowing that you have given your all.

Now that we understand the importance of putting icing in your work, let's look at some strategies on how to do it:

1.	The main key is dedication to excellence. Don't settle for the least effort. Always try to exceed expectations, go the extra mile, and give your all in every task you tackle.

2.	Putting icing in your work requires passion and commitment. When you love what you do, you are naturally inclined to devote yourself more vigorously and try to do your best.

3.	Be creative and look for innovative ways to meet challenges. Don't be afraid to think outside the box and come up with new ideas.

4.	Details make a difference. Take the time to refine the details of your work, whether it is a presentation, a report, or a project.

5.	Listen carefully to feedback from others and use this information to improve your work. Feedback is a valuable tool for learning and growth. If by chance you have done a job for a supervisor or colleague of yours, after you have performed the task , ask how the job was, what it is like to work with you or what you can improve the next time you are asked to do similar work. Never get tired of improving because until you do you can never get to the next level.

6. Never stop learning and growing. Constantly seek professional and personal development opportunities to hone your skills and expand your knowledge.

7. Work well in teams and collaborate effectively with others. Collaboration can lead to better and more satisfying results.

8. Meet deadlines and keep promises. This shows your reliability and dedication to your work.

9. Communicate clearly and effectively. Communication is critical to getting the value of your work across to others.

10. Don't neglect your personal well-being. Good physical and mental health helps you maintain the energy and focus you need to put some icing on your work.

11. Don't neglect your workplace. Beautify your workplace, create a clean, healthy and fragrant environment. Create a place where everyone feels comfortable and has the pleasure of returning.

Below I want to tell you the story of Andrea, an executive assistant at a veterinary practice, and how she went about putting frosting in her work.

Andrea was the executive assistant to a close-knit veterinarian, Dr. M. G. Her passion for animals was palpable in every aspect of her work. She didn't just answer client calls and schedule appointments, but constantly put frosting into her work to ensure exceptional service.

One day, a desperate woman showed up at the clinic with an injured stray puppy. Andrea greeted her calmly and kindly, reassuring her and recognizing the anxiety in her eyes. Immediately she took the puppy to the emergency area, where Dr. M. G and his team took care of the little patient. Andrea, meanwhile, stayed with the woman, providing her with emotional support and explaining the treatment process.

When the puppy was stable, Andrea took the time to help the woman fill out the necessary paperwork and explain the available payment options. The woman was moved by Andrea's compassion and dedication. In that moment, Andrea understood that her role was not just to handle the administrative aspects, but to make the customer experience as positive as possible.

Over the next few days, Andrea continued to track the puppy's progress and keep the woman informed. When the puppy was finally ready to be adopted, Andrea helped the woman find a loving family.

The story of the stray puppy quickly spread among the clinic's clients. Word of mouth about Andrea and her exceptional customer service reached Dr. M. G, who was deeply grateful for her assistant's extraordinary contribution. That day marked a turning point for Andrea. She realized that she could put icing in her work in ways that went beyond her daily responsibilities. She began to look for opportunities to surprise and delight clients, to always be ready to listen to their concerns and to offer her support.

As time went on, the clinic's reputation grew significantly because of the extraordinary client care provided by Andrea. Clients returned regularly and recommended the clinic to friends and family. Dr. M. G knew that he had a treasure in Andrea, an executive assistant who really put icing in her work, making every visit to the clinic a special and positive experience for clients and their beloved animals.

In conclusion, putting frosting in your work, just as Andrea did, is a practice that can lead to extraordinary results. It is the art of standing out with excellence, exceeding expectations and creating a lasting impression. It is a quality that can be developed by anyone in any professional field. Remember that your work is a reflection of yourself, and adding that extra touch can make the difference between success and mediocrity.

Chapter 11

Stories of Success

The Rise of Determination: The Story of Maria, Successful Executive Assistant

Maria was never the most self-confident person. Growing up in a modest family, she had always dreamed of getting a stable job that would allow her to support herself and her family. In 2008, Maria was hired as an executive assistant at a small financial consulting firm. At first, it seemed like just another job, but what was supposed to be a temporary job turned into an extraordinary story of success and personal revenge.

Maria entered the office world with little experience or self-esteem. She was introverted and often had difficulty being noticed. Her first task consisted mainly of ordering documents and answering the telephone. However, it was the beginning of a long and determined ascent.

Maria soon realized that in order to progress she needed to acquire new skills. She enrolled in evening classes in business administration and learned all she could about her company and the financial sector. Her dedication did not go unnoticed and she began to get involved in more complex projects.

In 2012, one rainy day, Maria got the opportunity that would change her life. The general manager asked her to prepare a presentation for an important client. Maria worked day and night to deliver a high-quality presentation. That presentation impressed the client, who chose to work with the company. This success attracted the attention of corporate executives.

Maria began to gain self-confidence. She had overcome challenges and proved her worth. Her personal revenge had begun. She began to actively participate in meetings and share her ideas. Her voice had weight and her opinions were heard.

In 2015, after years of hard work and commitment, Maria was promoted to administrative supervisor. It was a position of increased responsibility, but Maria was ready for it. She had demonstrated her ability to adapt and learn quickly. She successfully managed a team of secretaries and helped improve business processes.

Maria's growth was not without obstacles. In a male-dominated work environment, Maria felt isolated and sometimes ignored. However, instead of letting it get her down, she used this challenge as additional motivation to prove her worth.

With her new role comes increased stress and responsibility. Maria learned the importance of finding a balance between work and personal life. She began practicing yoga and devoting time to her family and personal interests.

Maria became a role model for her colleagues and a model of effective leadership. She was appreciated for her empathy, listening skills, and problem solving. She had become an example of determination and perseverance.

In 2020, after more than a decade with the company, Maria announced her decision to retire. She left a legacy of success and inspiration for her colleagues. The company continued to thrive because of the solid foundation she had helped build.

Even in retirement, Maria never stopped looking for new challenges. She devoted herself to volunteer work, helping other people develop their skills and find self-confidence.

Maria's story is an example of determination, personal growth and success through hard work and resilience. Through her personal revenge, she has shown that challenges can be overcome and success can be achieved, regardless of initial circumstances. Her story is an inspiration to anyone seeking to realize their dreams and achieve professional success.

The Executive Assistant Who Turned a Criticism into Success

Sarah, once an executive assistant at a prestigious law firm, had originally dreamed of becoming a lawyer. However, after a blow she suffered when she failed the law school entrance exam, she decided to pursue her passion in a different way. He joined the law firm as an executive assistant, but his aspiration remained intact.

Despite her unwavering commitment and dedication to her work, some colleagues regarded her only as "administrative support" with no real legal ambitions. This attitude could easily demoralize anyone, but Sarah had an inner strength that drove her to pursue her goal. When one of the lawyers openly criticized her, questioning her ability to become a lawyer, instead of letting it get her down, she turned that criticism into a flame of determination.

Sarah began to study with renewed vigor, devoting late nights and weekends to preparing for the admission test. She enrolled in evening law classes, absorbing every piece of information she could. In addition to her daily administrative work, she actively sought more complex legal projects and additional responsibilities to demonstrate her commitment and legal skills. He was not content to be just an executive assistant; he was building the foundation for his future as a lawyer.

After years of hard work and sacrifice, Sarah eventually passed the law school entrance exam. The joy and satisfaction she felt at that moment was immense. Finally, she had opened the door to her dream. She transferred to law school and began the path to her new career as a lawyer.

Her time spent as an executive assistant was not in vain; rather, it provided her with valuable practical skills, a unique insight into the workings of the law firm, and the determination to meet the challenges of lawyering. By the time she returned to the law firm as a lawyer, she had not only fulfilled her dream, she had proven to everyone that her role as executive assistant was not a limitation, but a stepping stone to a successful career in the legal field.

Her personal revenge was complete when her once skeptical former colleagues saw her in action as a successful lawyer. Sarah had not only demonstrated her legal competence but also gained the respect and esteem of her colleagues. Her story is an extraordinary example of determination, perseverance, and self-assertion, showing that with commitment and dedication, it is possible to turn even the fiercest criticism into an incredible stepping stone to success.

From the Stacks to the Stars

Melissa's remarkable story. is a testament to determination, personal growth and professional success. Starting from humble beginnings, she transformed her life and career from "stables" to "stars" through hard work, perseverance and a constant quest for improvement.

Melissa was born in a small Midwestern town into a modest family. From a young age, she had great ambition and a thirst for knowledge. Her indefatigable spirit and desire to overcome her family's economic hardships drove her to excel in school, earning scholarships that enabled her to enter higher education.

After graduating with a degree in foreign languages, Melissa began looking for work. However, she realized that the job market was competitive and that her initial expectations were unrealistic. She took a job as an executive assistant in a local small business. Despite her humble beginning, she met the challenge with commitment and determination.

In the early years of her career, Melissa performed basic tasks such as answering phones, arranging appointments, and handling correspondence. But she did not stop there. She was hungry for knowledge and wanted to grow professionally. She began studying secretarial best practices, took online courses, and read books on personal and professional development. She acquired advanced skills in document management, meeting organization and effective communication.

Her dedication began to pay off. Melissa has become a benchmark for the organization. Her ability to remain calm under pressure, solve problems creatively and maintain flawless communication caught the attention of her superiors. She was promoted to an executive assistant manager role, working directly with the company's CEO..

With this new position, Melissa faced even greater challenges. She had to manage busy calendars, plan complex corporate travel, and prepare detailed reports. The pressure was high, but she never gave up. She developed advanced skills in time management and task prioritization, ensuring that the CEO was always well prepared for meetings and engagements.

But her growth did not stop there. Melissa continued to improve herself. She took leadership courses and learned how to manage staff, becoming a mentor to young colleagues. She was respected not only for her professional skills, but also for her humility and ability to inspire others.

After several years of outstanding service, Melissa was promoted again, this time to a position of senior administrative coordinator. She was responsible for supervising the entire secretarial team and managing administrative operations. She had become a key member of the company's leadership team.

But her personal growth story was not just about her career. Meanwhile, she had invested in herself in many ways. She had learned to manage stress better through meditation and regular physical activity. She had also established a healthy work-life balance, devoting time to family, art, and her passion for volunteering.

Melissa had a clear vision for the future. She began to develop entrepreneurial skills and dreamed of creating her own secretarial consulting business. With her reputation in the industry and her extensive network of contacts, she was able to successfully launch her business.

Today, Melissa is a world-renowned executive assistant, trusted advisor to many Fortune 500 companies, and motivational speaker. She has written a successful book on personal growth and founded a charitable foundation that supports education in low-income communities.

Melissa's story is an extraordinary example of how determination, personal growth and hard work can transform a life and a career. From her humble beginning as an executive assistant, she has become an inspirational figure to many people around the world. Her story shows that it doesn't matter where you start, but how much you are willing to invest in yourself and how determined you are to achieve your goals. Melissa truly went from the "stalls" to the "stars" and proved that success is within reach for anyone with the will to pursue it.

CONCLUSIONS

Dearest Reader,

Having arrived at this point, I sincerely hope that you have found this guide not only useful but also inspiring in your professional journey. It has been a journey through the fundamental skills and knowledge that define a successful executive assistant, and together we have explored in depth the key aspects of this fascinating and challenging profession.

Now I would like to share a special wish with you. I sincerely hope that the future ahead of you is illuminated by the spotlight of success and personal fulfillment. I know that you have acquired the skills and knowledge necessary to face any challenge with confidence, thanks to the pages of this book. I hope that you can apply these skills effectively in your career, and that they can be the key to unlocking extraordinary opportunities.

Know that the role of an executive assistant has never been limited to administrative tasks; it is a multifunctional role that requires time management skills, communication, organization, and many other talents. With your commitment, you will be able to become an invaluable asset to your team and organization. Your skills will be the foundation on which you build a successful career and a reputation for reliability and professionalism.

Always remember the importance of continuous learning. Knowledge is an inexhaustible resource, and in the ever-changing world in which we live, it is essential to stay current on the latest trends and technologies. Keep looking for learning opportunities, attend classes and workshops, and keep your spirit curious and alive. This is the key to staying on top of an increasingly competitive job market.

As you seek to grow professionally, never forget to nurture your personal well-being as well. The work-life balance is crucial to maintaining a healthy level of energy and motivation. Take time for yourself, practice self-care, and enjoy life's little joys. These moments of respite can fuel your creativity and commitment to work.

Finally, remember that success is not just a destination, but an ongoing journey. Every challenge you face, every obstacle you overcome, and every goal you achieve will help define your personal success. Always be open to new opportunities and ready to grow from the challenge. Never allow temporary failures to obscure your vision of long-term success. Love your work, and you will not work a single day in your entire life. Love what you do, put your icing, passion and heart into it.

In conclusion, I sincerely wish you a bright and prosperous future professionally. May the skills taught in this guide prove decisive in your journey, and may you look back with pride and gratitude for all that you have accomplished. Keep growing, learning and pursuing your dreams with passion and determination. It will be your commitment and dedication that will shape your destiny, and I have no doubt that the future is bright and promising for you.

With sincerest wishes for success and happiness,

Jhonny R. Ross

www.ingramcontent.com/pod-product-compliance
Lightning Source LLC
Chambersburg PA
CBHW062348290526
45794CB00005B/2144